MARY WELLS LAWRENCE THE PIONEERING ADVERTISING EXECUTIVE

REVOLUTIONARY ADVERTISING JOURNEY

EMILY CYRUS

Disclaimer

This biography of Mary Wells Lawrence is a work of admiration and extensive research by the independent publisher Emily Cyrus.

While efforts have been made for accuracy, some creative elements have been added.

Mary Wells Lawrence and associates have not endorsed this work. It aims to inspire and celebrate her incredible impact.

Table of Contents

INTRODUCTION

Mary Wells Lawrence is a pioneering figure in the advertising industry, whose innovative approaches revolutionized the way products were marketed and brands were built. With a combination of creativity, strategic thinking, and fearlessness, she left an indelible mark on the world of advertising, shaping the landscape for generations to come.

Mary Wells Lawrence's significance in the advertising industry stems from her groundbreaking work that challenged traditional norms and redefined the art of persuasion. As one of the first female advertising executives to achieve widespread recognition, she shattered glass ceilings and paved the way for women in a predominantly male-dominated field.

Widely regarded as a visionary, Mary Wells Lawrence was a driving force behind some of the most iconic advertising campaigns of the 20th century.

Her agency, Wells Rich Greene, became synonymous with creativity, innovation, and effectiveness, setting new standards for advertising excellence.

One of Mary Wells Lawrence's most notable contributions was her emphasis on the "big idea" – a concept that transcended mere product features to tap into universal human emotions and aspirations. This approach revolutionized advertising by focusing on storytelling and emotional connection, rather than just selling products.

Mary Wells Lawrence was a trailblazer in the use of celebrity endorsements, employing cultural icons such as the Beatles and Liz Taylor to promote her clients' brands. Her ability to leverage popular culture and tap into the zeitgeist helped her campaigns resonate with audiences on a profound level.

Beyond her creative genius, Mary Wells Lawrence was also a savvy businesswoman and a charismatic leader. Under her guidance, Wells Rich Greene became one of the most successful advertising agencies of its time, garnering numerous awards and accolades for its groundbreaking work.

Mary Wells Lawrence was born on May 25, 1928, in Youngstown, Ohio. Raised in a middle-class family, she developed a passion for advertising at an early age, often drawing inspiration from the ads she saw in magazines and newspapers.

After graduating from high school, Mary Wells Lawrence attended the Carnegie Institute of Technology (now Carnegie Mellon University), where she studied advertising and graphic design. Armed with a keen intellect and a creative spirit, she quickly made a name for herself in the competitive world of Madison Avenue.

In 1953, Mary Wells Lawrence landed her first job in advertising as a copywriter at McCann Erickson. Over the next decade, she honed her craft and rose through the ranks, earning a reputation for her sharp wit and innovative thinking.

In 1966, Mary Wells Lawrence made history by co-founding Wells Rich Greene, a pioneering advertising agency that would revolutionize the industry. As the agency's president and creative director, she spearheaded some of the most iconic campaigns of the era, including "I ♥ New York" and "Plop, plop, fizz, fizz, oh what a relief it is" for Alka-Seltzer.

Throughout her career, Mary Wells Lawrence broke down barriers and defied expectations, proving that creativity knows no bounds. Her legacy continues to inspire generations of advertisers, reminding us that with passion, perseverance, and a dash of creativity, anything is possible.

CHAPTER 1

EARLY LIFE AND INFLUENCES

Mary was born Mary Georgene Berg on May 25, 1928, in Youngstown, Ohio to Fred and Rose Berg. She came from a middle-class Jewish family. Her father Fred worked as a manufacturer's representative selling aluminum products, while her mother Rose was a homemaker. She had one younger brother, Burt Berg. Her parents instilled a strong work ethic in her from an early age.

Mary attended Youngstown State University but dropped out after two years. She took her first job as a tour guide at the Yankee Girl Fried Chicken restaurant chain.

This exposed her to the power of branding and marketing. In 1949, she moved to New York City and landed a job as a secretary at an advertising agency, gaining her first experience in the ad world.

A major influence was her mentor, Freddie Niles, who ran the Yankee Girl Fried Chicken chain. He taught her about the importance of a consistent brand image. Another key influence was her first husband, Harding Lawrence, who encouraged her interest in advertising. Working as a lowly secretary exposed her to the sexism women faced, fueling her drive to make it in the male-dominated ad industry against the odds.

CHAPTER 2
CAREER BEGINNINGS

Mary Wells Lawrence's career in advertising began in humble circumstances, but she quickly rose through the ranks due to her talent, determination, and innovative marketing approach. Her early experiences laid the foundation for her eventual groundbreaking success as the first woman to own and run a major national advertising agency.

After dropping out of Youngstown State University, Mary took her first job as a tour guide at the Yankee Girl Fried Chicken restaurant chain in 1946. It was here that she gained her initial exposure to the power of branding and marketing under the tutelage of her mentor, Freddie Niles, who ran the chain.

Niles taught her the importance of maintaining a consistent brand image, a lesson that would prove invaluable in her future career.

Eager to explore opportunities beyond her small hometown, Mary made the bold decision to move to New York City in 1949. Despite having no connections in the big city, she managed to land a job as a secretary at an advertising agency, marking her official entry into the industry. While her role was low-level, it provided her with a front-row seat to the inner workings of the advertising world, allowing her to observe and learn from the creative minds around her.

It was during this time that Mary encountered the rampant sexism and discrimination that women faced in the male-dominated advertising industry. Rather than being deterred, these experiences fueled her determination to rise above the obstacles and make a name for herself in a field that was largely closed off to women.

Her first husband, Harding Lawrence, whom she married in 1951, played a pivotal role in supporting and encouraging her burgeoning interest in advertising. He recognized her talent and drive, and his unwavering belief in her abilities gave her the confidence to pursue her ambitions.

In the early years of her career, Mary took on various roles in advertising agencies, gaining valuable experience and honing her skills. One of her earliest successes came when she was tasked with reviving the faltering brand of Samsonite, the luggage company. Her innovative "Samsonite Furry Friends" campaign, featuring whimsical animal characters, was a hit and helped to breathe new life into the brand.

However, Mary's path to success was not without its challenges. As a woman in a male-dominated field, she faced constant discrimination and was often overlooked for promotions and leadership roles. Nevertheless, she persevered, working tirelessly to prove her worth and deliver exceptional results for her clients.

One of her most significant early achievements was her work on the "Plop, Plop, Fizz, Fizz" campaign for Alka-Seltzer. The catchy jingle and memorable imagery helped to establish Alka-Seltzer as a household name and cemented Mary's reputation as a creative force to be reckoned with in the advertising world.

Despite her successes, Mary encountered frustration at the lack of opportunities for advancement within the traditional agency structure. Determined to break through the glass ceiling, she made the bold decision to strike out on her own, establishing her agency, Wells Rich Greene, in 1966.

Mary's early career was marked by a relentless drive, a keen creative vision, and an unwavering determination to succeed in an industry that often tried to hold her back. Through her perseverance and talent, she paved the way for future generations of women in advertising, proving that success was possible even in the face of formidable obstacles.

CHAPTER 3

FOUNDING WELLS RICH GREENE

Founding Wells Rich Greene

In 1966, Mary Wells Lawrence made the groundbreaking decision to establish her advertising agency, Wells Rich Greene, in a move that defied the conventions of the male-dominated industry at the time.

This bold step not only allowed her to break free from the constraints and discrimination she faced within the traditional agency structure but also enabled her to reshape the very landscape of advertising.

The founding of Wells Rich Greene was a testament to Mary's unwavering determination and her refusal to accept the limitations imposed upon her by a system that favored men. Having witnessed firsthand the rampant sexism and glass ceiling that hindered the advancement of women in the industry, she was driven to create an agency that would embody her progressive values and empower talented individuals, regardless of gender.

To bring her vision to life, Mary assembled a team of like-minded professionals who shared her passion for innovative and impactful advertising. Among her first hires were Bill Rich and Walter Greene, two seasoned creatives who would lend their names to the agency. Together, they formed a dynamic trio that would go on to create some of the most iconic and influential campaigns of the era.

From the outset, Mary sought to cultivate an environment that fostered creativity, collaboration, and a sense of ownership among her employees. She believed that by empowering her team and encouraging them to take risks, they would produce work that resonated with audiences and effectively communicated the essence of each brand they represented.

The founding of Wells Rich Greene was not without its challenges. As a woman breaking into the upper echelons of a male-dominated industry, Mary faced skepticism and resistance from those who doubted her ability to lead a successful agency. However, her unwavering commitment to her vision and her exceptional talent quickly silenced her critics and paved the way for her agency's meteoric rise.

In the early years, Mary and her team took on a diverse array of clients, ranging from established brands to upstart companies seeking to make their mark. Their approach was bold, unconventional, and often provocative, challenging the status quo and pushing the boundaries of what was considered acceptable in advertising at the time.

One of the agency's earliest successes was the "I ♥ NY" campaign, which not only revitalized the image of New York City but also became a cultural phenomenon, transcending its original purpose as a marketing campaign. The iconic logo and slogan, designed by Milton Glaser, captured the essence of the city's resilience and vibrancy, resonating with audiences worldwide and cementing Wells Rich Greene's reputation as a creative powerhouse.

As the agency grew, Mary remained steadfast in her commitment to nurturing talent and fostering an environment that celebrated diversity and inclusivity. She recognized that by bringing together individuals from diverse backgrounds and perspectives, her agency would be better equipped to create work that resonated with a broad range of audiences.

The founding of Wells Rich Greene was not merely a milestone in Mary Wells Lawrence's career; it was a transformative moment in the history of advertising, shattering glass ceilings and challenging the industry's long-standing norms.

Through her visionary leadership and unwavering determination, Mary paved the way for future generations of women and minorities to pursue their ambitions in a field that had long been dominated by men.

Vision and Mission of Wells Rich Greene

At the core of Wells Rich Greene was a bold and progressive vision that challenged the conventions of the advertising industry and sought to redefine the agency's role in shaping cultural narratives. Under the visionary leadership of Mary Wells Lawrence, the agency's mission was not merely to create impactful campaigns but to foster an environment that celebrated creativity, diversity, and innovation.

Mary's vision for Wells Rich Greene was rooted in her belief that advertising had the power to transcend its commercial purpose and serve as a catalyst for social change. She recognized that by crafting narratives that resonated with audiences on a deeper level, her agency could not only promote brands but also shape perceptions, challenge societal norms, and inspire conversations around important issues.

One of the key pillars of Wells Rich Greene's mission was to cultivate an environment that empowered its employees and encouraged them to take risks. Mary understood that true creativity thrived in an atmosphere where individuals felt valued, supported, and free to explore unconventional ideas without fear of judgment or repercussions.

To achieve this, she fostered a collaborative culture that broke down traditional hierarchies and encouraged open dialogue among all members of the team. She believed that by bringing together diverse perspectives and voices, the agency would be better equipped to create work that resonated with a wide range of audiences, transcending cultural barriers and connecting with people on a fundamental level.

Another core aspect of Wells Rich Greene's mission was its commitment to championing diversity and inclusivity. Mary recognized that the advertising industry had long been dominated by a homogeneous group of individuals, which often resulted in campaigns that failed to resonate with marginalized communities.

By assembling a team that reflected the rich tapestry of society, Wells Rich Greene aimed to create work that was not only culturally relevant but also challenged stereotypes and celebrated the unique experiences of underrepresented groups.

Moreover, Wells Rich Greene sought to redefine the agency's role in shaping cultural narratives. Mary believed that advertising had the power to not only sell products but also to shape societal perceptions and catalyze conversations around important issues. This mission was exemplified in campaigns like "I ❤ NY," which transcended its commercial purpose and became a symbol of resilience and civic pride, resonating with audiences worldwide.

At the heart of Wells Rich Greene's vision and mission was an unwavering commitment to excellence, innovation, and social responsibility. Mary Wells Lawrence understood that by creating an environment that fostered creativity, celebrated diversity, and prioritized meaningful storytelling, her agency could not only produce groundbreaking work but also contribute to the broader cultural landscape in a profound and lasting way.

Through her bold leadership and unwavering commitment to her vision, Mary paved the way for a new generation of advertising agencies that sought to challenge the status quo and redefine the industry's role in shaping cultural narratives. Wells Rich Greene's mission was not merely to sell products but to inspire, provoke, and foster a more inclusive and socially conscious approach to advertising.

Key Projects and Campaigns at Wells Rich Greene

Under the visionary leadership of Mary Wells Lawrence, Wells Rich Greene established itself as a creative powerhouse, producing some of the most iconic and influential advertising campaigns of the era. From revitalizing the image of New York

City to challenging societal norms, the agency's work left an indelible mark on the industry and the broader cultural landscape.

One of the agency's most celebrated achievements was the "I ♥ NY" campaign, which not only revitalized the image of New York City but also became a cultural phenomenon that transcended its original purpose as a marketing campaign. The iconic logo and slogan, designed by Milton Glaser, captured the essence of the city's resilience and vibrancy, resonating with audiences worldwide and cementing Wells Rich Greene's reputation as a creative force to be reckoned with.

Another groundbreaking campaign that exemplified the agency's innovative approach was the "Plop, Plop, Fizz, Fizz" ad for Alka-Seltzer. By creating a catchy jingle and memorable imagery, Wells Rich Greene helped to establish Alka-Seltzer as a household name and set a new standard for creative excellence in the industry.

In addition to its work for iconic brands like Alka-Seltzer and New York City, Wells Rich Greene also took on a diverse array of clients, ranging from established companies to upstart brands seeking to make their mark. One such client was the American Telephone and Telegraph Company (AT&T), for whom the agency created the "Reach Out and Touch Someone" campaign. This emotionally resonant campaign not only helped to humanize the telecommunications giant but also tapped into the universal desire for human connection, solidifying Wells Rich Greene's reputation for crafting narratives that resonated with audiences on a deeper level.

Another noteworthy campaign was the agency's work for the American Indian Movement, which aimed to challenge stereotypes and raise awareness about the struggles faced by Native American communities. By leveraging the power of advertising to amplify marginalized voices and foster conversations around important social issues, Wells Rich Greene demonstrated its commitment to using its platform for more than just commercial gain.

In the realm of fashion and beauty, Wells Rich Greene made its mark with campaigns for brands like Braniff International Airlines and Max Factor Cosmetics. For Braniff, the agency created a series of advertisements that celebrated the airline's bold and vibrant brand identity, featuring striking visuals and innovative design elements that set a new standard for advertising in the travel industry.

Meanwhile, the agency's work for Max Factor Cosmetics challenged traditional notions of beauty and empowered women to embrace their individuality. The "Makeup

That Makes You Look Like You" campaign celebrated diversity and encouraged women to express themselves through makeup, rather than conforming to societal beauty standards.

Beyond its groundbreaking campaigns, Wells Rich Greene also played a pivotal role in shaping the industry's approach to talent development and diversity. Mary Wells Lawrence's commitment to nurturing creativity and fostering an inclusive environment inspired a new generation of advertising professionals, paving the way for greater representation and diverse perspectives within the industry through its innovative campaigns, socially conscious initiatives, and commitment.

CHAPTER 4
REVOLUTIONARY ADVERTISING STRATEGIES

Under the visionary leadership of Mary Wells Lawrence, Wells Rich Greene pioneered a revolutionary approach to advertising that challenged industry norms and redefined the way brands connect with audiences.

By embracing bold creativity, cutting-edge techniques, and a commitment to authenticity, the agency produced campaigns that not only resonated with consumers but also left an indelible mark on popular culture.

Innovations in Advertising Techniques:
One of the hallmarks of Wells Rich Greene's revolutionary strategies was its willingness to experiment with new advertising techniques and mediums. At a time when

television was emerging as a dominant force in advertising, the agency embraced the medium's potential for storytelling and emotional resonance.

Rather than relying solely on traditional product-focused advertisements, Wells Rich Greene crafted narratives that tapped into the human experience, creating emotional connections with audiences. This approach was exemplified in campaigns like "Reach Out and Touch Someone" for AT&T, which leveraged the power of human connection to humanize the telecommunications giant.

In addition to its innovative use of television, Wells Rich Greene also pushed boundaries in print advertising. The agency's campaigns often featured striking visuals, bold typography, and unconventional design elements that challenged the conventions of the time. This avant-garde approach not only captured attention but also reflected the agency's commitment to creativity and innovation.

Another area where Wells Rich Greene excelled was in the integration of advertising across multiple platforms. Recognizing the potential of a cohesive brand experience, the agency developed campaigns that seamlessly blended print, television, and emerging mediums like outdoor advertising and event marketing. This holistic approach ensured that brands maintained a consistent and impactful presence across various touchpoints, reinforcing their message and resonating with audiences on a deeper level.

In the realm of fashion and beauty, Wells Rich Greene made its mark with campaigns for brands like Braniff International Airlines and Max Factor Cosmetics. The agency's work for Braniff celebrated the airline's bold and vibrant brand identity, featuring striking visuals and innovative design elements that set a new standard for advertising in the travel industry.

Meanwhile, the "Makeup That Makes You Look Like You" campaign for Max Factor Cosmetics challenged traditional notions of beauty and empowered women to embrace their individuality. By celebrating diversity and encouraging self-expression, the campaign not only resonated with consumers but also reflected Wells Rich Greene's commitment to using advertising as a platform for social change and cultural impact.

Beyond its groundbreaking campaigns, Wells Rich Greene's revolutionary strategies extended to its approach to talent development and diversity. Mary Wells Lawrence's commitment to nurturing creativity and fostering an inclusive environment inspired a new generation of advertising professionals, paving the way for greater representation and diverse perspectives within the industry.

The agency's revolutionary strategies not only produced iconic campaigns but also challenged the industry's status quo, redefining the role of advertising in shaping cultural narratives and driving social change. By embracing bold creativity, cutting-edge techniques, and a commitment to authenticity, Wells Rich Greene left an indelible mark on the advertising landscape and set a new standard for agencies seeking to connect with audiences in meaningful and impactful ways.

CHAPTER 5
LEADERSHIP AT WELLS RICH GREENE

At the helm of Wells Rich Greene, Mary Wells Lawrence pioneered a leadership approach that defied traditional advertising industry norms. Her management style and philosophy were rooted in a belief that fostering an inclusive, collaborative, and nurturing environment was the key to unlocking creativity and producing groundbreaking work.

Management Style:
Mary's leadership style was characterized by a distinct lack of hierarchy and a willingness to challenge established systems. Unlike many of her contemporaries, she eschewed the rigid, top-down management structures that were prevalent in the advertising world at the time. Instead, she cultivated an environment that encouraged open

dialogue, collaboration, and a sense of ownership among her employees.

Central to Mary's approach was the belief that true creativity thrived when individuals felt empowered and valued. She understood that the best ideas often emerged from unexpected sources, and by fostering an atmosphere of trust and respect, she created an environment where every voice was heard and every perspective was considered.

Rather than dictating directives from an ivory tower, Mary preferred to lead by example. She was hands-on, actively engaging with her team, and embracing a collaborative approach to problem-solving. This level of accessibility not only fostered a sense of camaraderie within the agency but also allowed her to stay attuned to the challenges and concerns of her employees.

Another defining aspect of Mary's management style was her unwavering commitment to diversity and inclusivity. She recognized that the advertising industry had long been dominated by a homogeneous group of individuals, which often resulted in campaigns that failed to resonate with marginalized communities.

By actively seeking out and nurturing talent from diverse backgrounds, she ensured that Wells Rich Greene's work reflected a wide range of perspectives and experiences.

Philosophy:
At the core of Mary Wells Lawrence's leadership philosophy was a belief that advertising had the power to transcend its commercial purpose and serve as a catalyst for social change. She understood that by crafting narratives that resonated with audiences on a deeper level, her agency could not only promote brands but also shape perceptions, challenge societal norms, and inspire conversations around important issues.

This philosophy was reflected in the agency's groundbreaking campaigns, which often tackled sensitive subjects and challenged traditional advertising norms. From celebrating diversity in the "Makeup That Makes You Look Like You" campaign for Max Factor Cosmetics to raising awareness about the struggles faced by Native American communities, Wells Rich Greene's work reflected a commitment to using its platform for more than just commercial gain.

Moreover, Mary's philosophy emphasized the importance of authenticity and emotional resonance in advertising. She believed that by tapping into universal human experiences and creating narratives that connected with audiences on a visceral level, her agency could forge deeper connections between brands and consumers.

This approach was exemplified in campaigns like "Reach Out and Touch Someone" for AT&T, which leveraged the power of human connection to humanize the telecommunications giant and foster a sense of emotional resonance with audiences.

Underpinning Mary's philosophy was a deep respect for the power of creativity and a belief that true innovation could only flourish in an environment that celebrated risk-taking and encouraged individuals to push boundaries. She understood that the most groundbreaking work often emerged from unexpected places, and by fostering an atmosphere of experimentation and open-mindedness, she enabled her team to explore new frontiers in advertising.

Through her visionary leadership, Mary Wells Lawrence not only produced some of the most iconic and influential campaigns of the era but also reshaped the very landscape of the advertising industry. Her management style and philosophy challenged traditional norms, empowered her employees, and fostered an environment that celebrated diversity, authenticity, and the power of creativity to drive social change.

Company Culture and Values at Wells Rich Greene

At Wells Rich Greene, the company culture and values reflected the visionary leadership of Mary Wells Lawrence, who sought to create an environment that celebrated creativity, diversity, and a commitment to pushing boundaries. From its inception, the agency embodied a spirit of innovation and a willingness to challenge industry norms, setting it apart from its more traditional counterparts.

Culture:

Central to the culture at Wells Rich Greene was a sense of collaboration and open dialogue. Unlike many agencies of the time, which were characterized by rigid hierarchies and top-down decision-making, Mary fostered an atmosphere where every voice was heard and every perspective was valued. This inclusive approach not only fostered a sense of camaraderie among employees but also ensured that the agency's work reflected a diverse range of experiences and viewpoints.

Creativity was celebrated and encouraged at every level of the organization. Mary understood that true innovation often emerged from unexpected places, and by cultivating an environment that encouraged risk-taking and experimentation, she enabled her team to explore new frontiers in advertising.

The agency's physical spaces were designed to inspire creativity and facilitate collaboration. Open-plan workspaces and informal meeting areas encouraged spontaneous interactions and the free exchange of ideas, fostering an atmosphere of intellectual curiosity and creative exploration.

Values:

At the core of Wells Rich Greene's values was a commitment to authenticity and emotional resonance. The agency believed that truly impactful advertising went beyond simply promoting products or services; it tapped into universal human experiences and forged deeper connections with audiences.

This value was reflected in campaigns like "I ♥ NY" and "Reach Out and Touch Someone," which resonated with audiences on a visceral level and transcended their original commercial purposes to become cultural phenomena.

Diversity and inclusivity were also central to Wells Rich Greene's value system. Mary recognized that the advertising industry had long been dominated by a homogeneous group of individuals, which often resulted in campaigns that failed to resonate with marginalized communities. By actively seeking out and nurturing talent from diverse backgrounds, the agency ensured that its work reflected a wide range of perspectives and experiences, ultimately producing campaigns that resonated with audiences across cultural and demographic boundaries.

Wells Rich Greene embraced the value of social responsibility and a commitment to using its platform for more than just commercial gain. This was exemplified in campaigns like the agency's work for the American Indian Movement, which aimed to challenge stereotypes and raise awareness about the struggles faced by Native American communities.

Innovation and a willingness to push boundaries were also core values at Wells Rich Greene. The agency was never content to simply follow industry trends; instead, it sought to redefine the very role of advertising in shaping cultural narratives and driving social change.

This spirit of innovation manifested in the agency's groundbreaking use of new advertising techniques and mediums, as well as its avant-garde approach to design and visual storytelling.

Through its company culture and values, Wells Rich Greene embodied the revolutionary spirit of its founder, Mary Wells Lawrence.

By fostering an environment that celebrated creativity, diversity, and a commitment to pushing boundaries, the agency not only produced iconic campaigns but also reshaped the very landscape of the advertising industry, paving the way for a more inclusive, socially conscious, and innovative approach to advertising.

CHAPTER 6
PERSONAL AND PROFESSIONAL CHALLENGES

Mary Wells Lawrence's pioneering journey in the advertising industry was marked by numerous obstacles and challenges, both personal and professional. As a woman striving to make her mark in a male-dominated field, she faced systemic discrimination, gender bias, and entrenched societal norms that attempted to thwart her ambitions at every turn.

However, Mary's determination and resilience enabled her to overcome these formidable barriers and pave the way for future generations of women in advertising.

One of the most significant obstacles Mary faced was the pervasive sexism and gender discrimination that permeated the advertising industry during the mid-20th century. Despite her exceptional talent and creative prowess, she was often overlooked for promotions and leadership roles, with men being favored for advancement opportunities. This blatant discrimination not only hindered her professional growth but also served as a constant reminder of the deeply ingrained biases she was up against.

In addition to gender-based discrimination, Mary also encountered skepticism and doubt from those who questioned her ability to lead and succeed in a field dominated by men. Many dismissed her ambitions as mere fantasies, believing that a woman could never ascend to the upper echelons of the advertising industry. This pervasive lack of faith in her capabilities added a layer of challenge, as Mary had to continuously prove her worth and silence her detractors.

Another obstacle that Mary faced was the need for more female role models and mentors in the advertising industry. As one of the few women pursuing a career in this field, she had to navigate uncharted territory without the guidance and support of those who had walked a similar path. This absence of mentorship made her journey even more arduous, as she had to learn valuable lessons through trial and error, often facing setbacks and disappointments along the way.

Beyond the professional challenges, Mary also encountered personal obstacles that threatened to derail her ambitions. As a wife and mother, she had to juggle the demands of her career with the responsibilities of family life, a feat that was particularly challenging in an era when societal expectations placed a greater emphasis on women's domestic roles.

Despite these formidable obstacles, Mary remained steadfast in her pursuit of success, employing a range of strategies to overcome adversity and pave her path to the top.

Strategies for Overcoming Adversity:
One of Mary's most effective strategies was her belief in herself and her abilities. In the face of constant doubt and criticism, she refused to be deterred, maintaining an unshakable confidence in her creative talents and leadership potential. This self-assurance served as a powerful motivator, propelling her forward even when the odds seemed insurmountable.

Mary cultivated a support network of like-minded individuals who shared her vision and provided encouragement and guidance. By surrounding herself with a team of talented professionals who believed in her mission, she created an environment that fostered creativity, collaboration, and a sense of collective purpose.
Resilience and perseverance were also key strategies that enabled Mary to overcome

adversity. She understood that success rarely comes without setbacks and failures, and she embraced these challenges as opportunities for growth and learning. When faced with obstacles, she remained steadfast, adapting her approach and exploring new avenues to achieve her goals.

Mary recognized the importance of taking calculated risks and challenging established norms. Rather than conforming to the status quo, she boldly forged her path, breaking down barriers and redefining what was possible for a woman in the advertising industry. This willingness to push boundaries and disrupt traditional structures played a crucial role in her ultimate success.

Perhaps most importantly, Mary's commitment to excellence and her passion for her craft fueled her determination to overcome any obstacle that stood in her way. She understood that true greatness required unwavering dedication and an unyielding pursuit of perfection. This relentless drive propelled her forward, even in the face of daunting challenges and adversities.

Through her indomitable spirit, resilience, and innovative strategies, Mary Wells Lawrence not only overcame the formidable obstacles that threatened to derail her career but also blazed a trail for future generations of women in advertising and beyond. Her journey serves as a testament to the power of perseverance, self-belief, and the unwavering pursuit of one's dreams, even in the face of seemingly insurmountable adversity.

CHAPTER 7

After establishing Wells Rich Greene as a pioneering and influential force in the advertising industry, Mary Wells Lawrence's journey took a new turn as she transitioned out of the agency she had founded. Although she stepped away from the day-to-day operations of Wells Rich Greene, Mary's impact on the industry continued to reverberate through her ongoing contributions and advocacy for women in advertising.

Transition out of Wells Rich Greene:

In 1990, after nearly a quarter of a century at the helm of Wells Rich Greene, Mary decided to step down as the agency's president and chief executive officer. This transition marked the end of an era and a significant shift in her professional trajectory.

While the decision to leave the agency she had built from the ground up was undoubtedly difficult, Mary recognized that it was time to embark on a new chapter in her career. Over the years, she had faced numerous challenges and obstacles, including a highly publicized legal battle with the agency's parent company, which had taken a toll on her.

However, even as she stepped away from Wells Rich Greene, Mary remained deeply committed to the advertising industry and the ideals that had fueled her success. She understood that her journey had not only paved the way for future generations of women in advertising but had also reshaped the industry's approach to creativity, inclusivity, and social responsibility.

Continued Contributions to the Industry:
In the years following her departure from Wells Rich Greene, Mary Wells Lawrence

she continued to make significant contributions to the advertising industry, serving as a mentor, advocate, and source of inspiration for countless professionals.

One of her most notable initiatives was the establishment of the Mary Wells Lawrence Seminar at the University of Missouri's School of Journalism. This annual event brought together students, professionals, and industry leaders to explore the latest trends and challenges in advertising, while also fostering discussions around diversity, ethical practices, and the power of advertising to drive social change.

Through this seminar, Mary shared her wealth of knowledge and experience with the next generation of advertising professionals, imparting valuable lessons on creativity, leadership, and the importance of staying true to one's values and principles.

In addition to her work with the University of Missouri, Mary also served as a consultant and advisor to various agencies and organizations, lending her expertise and insights to help shape the future of the industry she had helped to transform.

Moreover, Mary's influence extended beyond the realm of advertising, as she became a sought-after speaker and author, sharing her remarkable story and inspiring others to pursue their dreams with unwavering determination and resilience. Her memoir, "A Big Life (in Advertising)," offered a candid and inspiring account of her journey, chronicling the challenges she faced and the strategies she employed to overcome adversity.

Through her writing and public speaking engagements, Mary continued to be a powerful advocate for women's empowerment and a champion of diversity and inclusivity within the advertising industry and beyond.

Even in her later years, Mary's passion for advertising and her commitment to driving positive change remained unwavering. She recognized that her journey had not only broken barriers but had also paved the way for future generations to pursue their dreams without the constraints of gender bias and discrimination.

In many ways, Mary Wells Lawrence's later career and achievements were a continuation of the groundbreaking work she had begun at Wells Rich Greene – a testament to her enduring legacy as a trailblazer, a visionary, and a true pioneer in the advertising industry.

CHAPTER 8

Mary Wells Lawrence's pioneering journey in the advertising industry left an indelible mark that continues to reverberate across generations. Her trailblazing spirit, innovative approach, and unwavering determination to shatter glass ceilings have cemented her legacy as a transformative force in the field of advertising and a champion of women's empowerment.

Mary Wells Lawrence's Lasting Influence on Advertising:

One of Mary's most enduring legacies is her role in redefining the very nature of advertising. Through her groundbreaking campaigns, she demonstrated the power of advertising to transcend its commercial purpose and serve as a catalyst for social change. Campaigns like "I ♥ NY" and "Reach Out and Touch Someone" not only resonated with audiences on an emotional level but also challenged societal norms and inspired conversations around important issues.

By embracing authenticity, emotional resonance, and a commitment to telling stories that reflected the human experience, Mary paved the way for a new era of advertising that prioritized meaningful connections over mere product promotion. Her approach has inspired countless agencies and professionals to adopt a more purpose-driven and socially conscious mindset, recognizing the potential of advertising to shape cultural narratives and drive positive change.

Mary's determination to foster an inclusive and diverse environment at Wells Rich Greene has had a lasting impact on the industry's approach to talent development and representation. By actively seeking out and nurturing talent from diverse backgrounds, she challenged the homogeneity that had long characterized the advertising world, paving the way for greater inclusivity and a more accurate reflection of the diverse audiences that brands seek to reach.

Her commitment to empowering women and breaking down gender barriers has also left an indelible mark. Mary's success as the first woman to own and run a major national advertising agency and the first female chief executive of a company listed on the New York Stock Exchange served as a powerful inspiration for generations of women aspiring to leadership roles in male-dominated industries.

By shattering glass ceilings and proving that women could achieve success at the highest levels, Mary's journey has inspired countless individuals to pursue their ambitions without limitations, challenging the entrenched biases and systemic discrimination that had long held women back.

Recognition and Honors Received:
In recognition of her groundbreaking achievements and lasting impact, Mary Wells Lawrence has been honored with numerous accolades and awards throughout her illustrious career and beyond.

In 1971, she became the first woman to be named Advertising Woman of the Year by the American Advertising Federation. This prestigious honor not only celebrated her professional accomplishments but also acknowledged her role as a trailblazer, paving the way for future generations of women in the industry.

Mary was also inducted into the Advertising Hall of Fame in 1999, a well-deserved recognition of her pioneering contributions to the field and her enduring legacy as a creative force and visionary leader.

Beyond the advertising industry, Mary's impact has also been recognized by esteemed institutions and organizations. In 2003, she received an honorary doctorate from the University of Missouri, recognizing her lifetime achievements and her ongoing commitment to nurturing the next generation of advertising professionals through the Mary Wells Lawrence Seminar.

Mary has been the recipient of numerous lifetime achievement awards, including the Matrix Award from New York Women in Communications and the Advertising Club of New York's prestigious Lifetime Achievement Award.

These honors and accolades not only celebrate Mary Wells Lawrence's professional accomplishments but also serve as a testament to the enduring impact of her legacy. Through her unwavering determination, innovative spirit, and commitment to empowering others, she has left an indelible mark on the advertising industry and beyond, inspiring countless individuals to pursue their dreams and challenge the status quo.

Mary's journey serves as a powerful reminder that true greatness often arises from the ability to overcome adversity and shatter barriers. Her legacy stands as a beacon of hope and inspiration, encouraging future generations to embrace their authenticity, celebrate diversity, and never underestimate the power of their voices to drive meaningful change.

CHAPTER 9

REFLECTIONS AND LESSONS

Mary Wells Lawrence's trailblazing career in the advertising industry is a wellspring of invaluable insights and lessons, both for aspiring professionals and established leaders in the field. Through her experiences navigating the male-dominated landscape of mid-20th-century advertising, Mary not only shattered glass ceilings but also imparted wisdom that continues to resonate across generations.

Insights from Mary Wells Lawrence's Experiences:

One of the most profound insights gleaned from Mary's journey is the transformative power of authenticity and emotional resonance in advertising. Throughout her career, she championed the idea that truly impactful campaigns go beyond mere product promotion and tap into universal human experiences. Her groundbreaking work, such as the "I ♥ NY" and "Reach Out and Touch Someone" campaigns, demonstrated the ability of advertising to forge deeper connections with audiences and shape cultural narratives.

Mary's experiences also underscore the importance of fostering a diverse and inclusive environment in the advertising industry. By actively seeking out and nurturing talent from diverse backgrounds, she ensured that her agency's work reflected a wide range of perspectives and experiences, ultimately producing campaigns that resonated with audiences across cultural and demographic boundaries.

Mary's journey serves as a testament to the power of perseverance and resilience in the face of adversity. As a woman striving to make her mark in a male-dominated field, she encountered numerous obstacles, including systemic discrimination, gender bias, and entrenched societal norms. However, her unwavering determination and self-belief enabled her to overcome these formidable barriers and pave the way for future generations of women in advertising.

Lessons for Aspiring Advertisers and Executives:

For aspiring professionals in the advertising industry, Mary Wells Lawrence's story offers invaluable lessons on the importance of cultivating a bold, innovative spirit and embracing risk-taking.

Throughout her career, Mary challenged established norms and pushed the boundaries of what was considered acceptable in advertising. Her willingness to disrupt traditional structures and explore uncharted territory played a crucial role in her success and continues to inspire a new generation of creatives to think outside the box.

Aspiring advertisers can also learn from Mary's commitment to excellence and her unwavering pursuit of perfection. She understood that true greatness required unwavering dedication and an unyielding drive to deliver exceptional work. This relentless pursuit of excellence not only fueled her success but also inspired those around her to strive for higher standards.

For executives and leaders in the advertising industry, Mary's experiences highlight the importance of creating a nurturing environment that fosters collaboration, open dialogue, and a sense of ownership among employees. By eschewing rigid hierarchies and embracing a collaborative approach, Mary cultivated an atmosphere where every voice was heard and every perspective was valued, ultimately leading to more innovative and impactful work.

Mary's leadership style underscores the value of leading by example and remaining accessible to one's team. Through her hands-on approach and willingness to engage directly with her employees, she fostered a sense of camaraderie and trust, enabling her to stay attuned to the challenges and concerns of those she led.

Perhaps one of the most enduring lessons from Mary Wells Lawrence's journey is the power of using one's platform for positive change. Throughout her career, she leveraged the influence of advertising to challenge societal norms, raise awareness about important issues, and inspire conversations around diversity, inclusivity, and social responsibility.

This commitment to purpose-driven advertising serves as a powerful reminder that the industry has the potential to shape cultural narratives and drive meaningful change.
In reflecting on Mary Wells Lawrence's pioneering journey, it is clear that her legacy

extends far beyond her professional achievements. Her experiences offer a wealth of wisdom and inspiration for aspiring professionals, executives, and leaders alike, reminding us of the transformative power of authenticity, inclusivity, perseverance, and a steadfast commitment to using one's voice for positive change.

CONCLUSION

Mary Wells Lawrence's life and career stand as a testament to the power of determination, creativity, and an unwavering commitment to breaking barriers. From her humble beginnings in Youngstown, Ohio, to her groundbreaking achievements as the first woman to own and run a major national advertising agency, Mary's journey has left an indelible mark on the advertising industry and inspired generations of women to pursue their dreams without limitations.

Throughout her pioneering career, Mary faced numerous obstacles, including systemic discrimination, gender bias, and entrenched societal norms that attempted to thwart her ambitions at every turn. However, her resilience, self-belief, and innovative spirit enabled her to overcome these formidable barriers and pave the way for future generations of women in advertising.

At the helm of Wells Rich Greene, Mary pioneered a revolutionary approach to advertising that celebrated authenticity, emotional resonance, and a commitment to using her platform for positive change. Her groundbreaking campaigns, such as "I ♥ NY" and "Reach Out and Touch Someone," not only achieved remarkable commercial success but also transcended their original purposes, becoming cultural phenomena that shaped societal perceptions and inspired conversations around important issues.

Mary's impact extended far beyond the realm of advertising, as she became a mentor, advocate, and source of inspiration for countless professionals. Through initiatives like the Mary Wells Lawrence Seminar at the University of Missouri's School of Journalism, she shared her wealth of knowledge and experience, nurturing the next generation of advertising professionals and imparting valuable lessons on creativity, leadership, and the power of staying true to one's values and principles.

In recognition of her groundbreaking achievements and lasting impact, Mary Wells Lawrence has been honored with numerous accolades and awards, including induction into the Advertising Hall of Fame and prestigious lifetime achievement awards. These honors not only celebrate her professional accomplishments but also serve as a testament to the enduring legacy of her trailblazing spirit and her commitment to empowering others.

As we reflect on Mary Wells Lawrence's extraordinary journey, it is clear that her legacy extends far beyond her professional achievements. Her experiences offer a wellspring of insights and lessons for aspiring professionals, executives, and leaders alike, reminding us of the transformative power of authenticity, inclusivity, perseverance, and a steadfast commitment to using one's voice for positive change.

Mary's journey serves as a powerful reminder that true greatness often arises from the ability to overcome adversity and shatter barriers. Her unwavering determination, innovative spirit, and commitment to fostering an inclusive and socially conscious environment have left an indelible mark on the advertising industry and beyond, inspiring countless individuals to embrace their authenticity, celebrate diversity, and never underestimate the power of their voices to drive meaningful change.

In the words of Mary Wells Lawrence herself, "If you think you can do a thing or think you can't do a thing, you're right." Her life and career are a living embodiment of this powerful sentiment, a testament to the extraordinary heights that can be achieved when one refuses to be limited by the constraints of societal norms or the doubts of others.

As we bid farewell to this extraordinary trailblazer, we are reminded of the enduring legacy she has left behind – a legacy that will continue to inspire generations to come, challenging them to dream big, break boundaries, and create a world where opportunity knows no gender, where diversity is celebrated, and where the power of advertising is harnessed to drive positive change.